HEALING WILL HAVE
YOU TRIPPIN'

HEALING WILL HAVE YOU Trippin'

I HEAL AS I WRITE

KISHNA MARIE

Foreword by Catherine Abrams BSN, RN

Kae-oh Publishing

Contents

ISBN: 978-1-7372797-0-9
eISBN: 978-1-7372797-1-6

Printed and Bound in the United States
First Printing, 2021

This book is dedicated to Katherine Marie Outlaw (granny), Edna Marie Taylor (great-grandmom), and Lydia Brown (grandmum). I finally stopped, I quieted, I heard, I let go, I acknowledged, and I bowed.

Epigraph

Trippin' (noun slang) - an illusion of
proceeding something that does not
really exist.

- Roget's II: The New
Thesaurus, 3rd Edition

Foreward

I am a registered nurse who has worked with the underserved population most of my career. One of the experiences which I have learned the most was when I worked with youth at a homeless shelter. A colleague of mine and I provided group therapy based on Dialectical Behavioral Therapy model along with the Community Resilience Model, which I am a certified teacher. I watched youth become more resilient and gain life skills from these support groups. It is the reaction to adversity, not the adversity itself, that determines how one's life story will develop. Watching others overcome their own trauma and adversities in life has given me strength, courage, and resiliency.

I met Kishna when I started a research job working as the nurse care-manger for a study involving people living with HIV who were on chronic opioid therapy. Kishna was the research assistant in this study. We instantly connected as we both believed in giving kindness and compassion to others especially those who have had lots of adversity in their lives. Soon after the study started, I faced my own adversity as my husband was diagnosed with pancreatic cancer. Kishna walked beside me during this difficult time, and she continued to walk beside me after he died. A lot of people do not know how to walk beside someone as they feel more comfortable trying to lead someone out of their pain. Kishna was comfortable to not only walk beside but also just sit with me and feel dark deep pain. She listened always with her heart and soul. I remember crying to her and could feel how comfortable she was to sit with me in my pain which allowed me to be more authentic and start to heal.

I believe Kishna is able to show loving-kindness and compassion as she not only understands emotional pain from everyday life, but she is a survivor of childhood trauma and adversity. She reacts to her adversity by healing from the inside out. Journaling was and continues to be a tool that is a large part of her healing. We both have shared our thoughts and entries that we have made in our own journals. Writing with pen and paper one's own thoughts has been proven to increase the ability to adapt and heal from adversity. Kishna healed and continues to heal using writing. Sharing her thoughts, feelings, and pain through this book, will help others on their journey to freedom.

I am also struck by her writing about sitting with her emotions, allowing space for them to be present and then move through her body. This is another example of how she is brave and whoever reads her book will gain insight into some skills to use for their own healing.

I am honored to write the forward to this book as Kishna's ability to share herself will give healing to others.

Love to all.….…...Catherine Abrams BSN, RN

Preface

This book is a compilation of freewriting, notes to me, and journal writings. In these writings, I share with you my journey through the course of my continuous healing process. Throughout this book, you will find lessons that are not fully digested, contradictions, imperishable truths, and a great many moments of resetting me.

My love of writing started at an early age. Writing was an escape from the chaos-filled world I was growing up in. Through writing I built an invisible layer of safety that I could rest in when I needed it. Writing has taken me on delightful adventures to places of joy and overwhelming peace that mirrored real moments of happiness that I experienced and, in my writings, exaggerated. I wanted the experience of these happy times to endure forever. For this reason, writing grounded me, it comforted me and gave me hope as a child. As I became older, writing gave me the space to sit with my feelings and write myself into a future of love, letting go, and healing.

Expressing myself through writing enlightens the way I see myself and others, teaching me the difference between joy and happiness. Writing is my safe space—it is where I found the art of being transparent and where my truth resides. The more I committed pen to paper the more I realized healing is not in the lies I tell myself but in the fear of the truth that I lay aside. I believe that with open dialogue, transparency, and truth I can help not only myself but everyone who reads this book to wake up to a life of true authenticity, bringing peace within you as it has done me. It has been my experience through healing that authenticity bridges the gap between stigma, shame, and love for self.

When I started living in my truth, the truth brought into existence an unusual sense of discernment for me. What I thought were obstacles were steppingstones leading to my purpose. The truth at times placed me in a state of mental suffering, forcing me to intentionally confront the past and move beyond the lies I was telling myself. In return, the love for myself has grown to unlock the freedom in me to not place others before me regardless of the circumstance. To give a firm "NO" in order to say yes to my mental well-being and not caring about the chitter-chatter of the masses. With all the seen and unseen scars, I fully awakened the energy within.

Acknowledgement

To Grey, my love, thank you for your patience, your time, your honesty, and your love. You gave me the space I needed to be alone to write and you held me when I was emotionally tired from feeling the words I had written. You celebrated every moment of healing with me just as we celebrate every moment of our life together. I love you G-R-E-Y. Us. Cheers to more moments.

To my sonshine-Timmy, you are my love, you are greatness, I saw it in you before I saw it in me. I will continue to speak greatness over you- your gifts are waiting for you.

To my dad, my father, Charlie Brown, thank you for being my everything and not giving up on me at my worst. You celebrated me and bragged about me at every single moment in my life. Thank you.

To my Christy Love (Mom),I miss you.

To the women of Dunleith the ones physically here and the ones who are not physically here, you are the best. Dunleith is historical in its own right, but when I talk about home, I talk about you. I took something from each and every one of you and I hold it close to my heart. At times I was too ashamed to talk about my trials, but you all in some way knew what I needed, it could have been a hug, to sit in quietness with the television on, reassurance, or just kind words, whatever it was you gave it to me. The most important point I need to mention is that none of you judged me for my healthy appetite. Thank you.

To my Sista's and my brotha's, thank you all for answering the numerous texts I sent out about this book. Thank you for not calling me out on my disappearing acts and being there when I would just show up with no warning. Thank you for believing in me and not leaving my side. Thank you for showing up for me when I could not budge. Thank you for your check-up's, they are appreciated.

To Catherine, thank you for writing that amazing Foreword. Thank you for sitting with me, walking with me, being my cheerleader, and taking the lead with me.

To the editor Carmen Smith thank you, are a great writing coach as well as an editor.

My Deepest Gratitude to all who have purchased this book.

1

WORDS CAN BE A BLESSING OR A CURSE

Words are not just words.
Words are not fleeting.
Words can be harming.
Words impaired me.
Words penetrated my soul.
Words are never just words.
Words can be haunting.
I feared words.
Words came to the forefront of my mind.

With every decision I made, it was those words that were said to me on which I decided.

So, I started using my words to forget the pain.

I formed my words into beautiful short stories and poetry describing how I saw beauty in others and the goodness I wished my world could be.

My words were soothing to my soul.

Those words were my escape, they held me, not like the harsh words that destroyed me. The words I wrote were similar to the words spoken to me on Popular Street by my granny and great grandmom.

From beyond the grave, I am reminded of the words they said to me. They spoke these words in a gentle, comforting tone that remained continually unchanged on each occasion, and on each occasion, these words came with tears welling up in their eyes, yet I saw not one teardrop. Their words gave me solace during the chaos. They spoke these words over me time and time again and to this very day I am not sure why their words did not permeate through me as the other harmful words did. Nevertheless, that is okay. I am aware now. Their presence is felt, and their words are now placed in between quotation marks as a reminder to me.

I AM the words my granny and great grandmom spoke over me.

I have released the words that cursed me and kept me bound.

I AM the love I was promised.

I AM the gift of a spiritual being.

I AM the sun that shines upon the earth.

I AM the moon who lightens the darkness.

I AM the darkness that needs the light.

I AM LOVE . . . FAITH . . . GOODNESS.

I AM THE CHANGE GRANNY AND GREAT GRANDMOM SPOKE OF.

I USE THE POWER OF *"I AM"* TO
CHANGE AND CREATE THE
LANDSCAPE OF MY MIND.

WITH EACH *"I AM"* NEW SEEDS
ARE PLANTED.

2

GENERATIONAL CURSES, LEARNED BEHAVIOR

I do not believe in generational curses. Do you? It is a learned behavior. It is something someone says so many times that you start to believe it, then become it, repeating the behavior of the last generation. Not knowing you do not have to believe or become it or repeat it. When one of my family members mentions anything about a generational curse, I dismiss them. I will never understand how one says that to another, giving them no hope to move on. To me, it is nonsense. We create our own path. I became aware that I would never have been able to get my mind right in an acidic environment.

I did not think it was okay to leave something I was part of, and I did not for a while. I could have left at eighteen with my son, but I thought I would be giving up on my own family, so I stayed. My favorite uncle left and never came back, living a happy and eventful life. I could not muster the strength, confidence, or courage to follow his lead on my own with a child.

Also, I was comfortable . . . I am not going to lie, but I was miserable. I gave more of myself, my time, and my money away hoping for a change in others. That did not work. My granny raised me to defy what was expected of me from her children. Of course, I never listened because I wanted to fit in with my surroundings. Now that sounds crazy—why should I have to fit in? This is where I am from, we all have a shared history, we have the same blood circulating through our veins. My granny (my roots) taught me to stand strong, be nice, and to move slowly. Do not tell anyone what you are planning, she said. I have learned now that those things are what give me power. The roots I grew from are strong. They pushed me to grow as strong as them in hopes of me surpassing them and branching off.

Another thing about some roots is that sometimes they get entangled, not spreading out into the soil, getting stunted, and seeming to stay small forever. This is what happens when the roots do not push you and give you easy options that they may have considered for themselves once upon a time instead of giving you hard choices for you to decide on, for growth, and to one day branch off with. They give you their options because, for them, it may have been all they had to choose from. Now you are taking their options and using them in your life, now staying entangled and sometimes strangling yourself for the sake of not being not left out of something you were born into.

The generational curse (when and if you believe in them) can be deep-rooted and grow wild in the form of normalized generational trauma.

CURSES ARE MADE TO BE BROKEN

3

TRIUMPH OVER TRAUMA

In growing in and through trauma, I was able to understand the complexity of generational trauma.

I acknowledged the generational trauma. I put a name to it, and I called it out. It was hidden in a life we normalized. I understood that I was living in it, and I had to get through it on my own. I had to ask myself, "Do I want to triumph over trauma?" That scared me.

"Do I really want to triumph over trauma?"

This sentence gave me chest pain, where my heart was beating so fast, I thought it was going to explode.

I like to be challenged even when frightened so I said "yes."

In understanding the complexity of generational trauma, I realized that being responsible for myself and forgiveness replaces any blame I placed on others to justify my own circumstances.

In understanding generational trauma, I knew I would no longer want to try and adjust myself to the standards or circumstances that created a refusal to acknowledge truth if we were perceived as "having it all together." I mirrored that for years, perpetuating a lifestyle that destroyed not only our family but our community from the inside out.

I came to the realization that I was losing myself and my son to these roles we were called to cast in. I did not have to answer that call, but I did. Luckily, my power to walk away was stronger than the power calling me to be perceived as "having it all together."

What is a beautiful smile if you are crying on the inside?

They said it was normal. They said it was a curse that plagued us generations back. They said this is our life.

I found that to be untrue. I chose to triumph over trauma, for I could not expect to arrive at who I was becoming if I did not recognize and cancel who "they" said I AM.

Let us all heal together and triumph over trauma. In case we never get that chance, I respect and accept that we are a part of each other and, being a part of each other, I hope you respect and accept the decisions I continue to make to break free of the generational trauma.

I NO LONGER NORMALIZE
TRAUMATIC EXPERIENCES
TRANSITIONING FROM
GENERATION TO GENERATION.

4

TRANSPARENCY

I was scared to be transparent.

I was scared to talk about past mistakes.

I was so used to being judged that transparency was not even a thought.

I was frightened to speak my thoughts, as I felt it would turn people away.

My thoughts made me cry.

I wanted to silence them as there were too many voices.

I yearned to speak my thoughts because I wanted help.

* * *

Psychologists worked but the unemotional faces made me think of how their faces must be tired of posing in resting face position all day. I thought give me a smile not a smirk and hold the smirk a little longer. They also must be tired of jotting irrelevant thoughts down on that boring paper with no lines to ask me after I finish talking. Plus, I would do them the favor of pausing so they could ask, "How did you feel about that?" I would leave relieved, knowing I released some thoughts but laughing because of that resting face and all that note writing.

* * *

I wanted to speak my truth to my peers.

When I talked to them, I did not want to think about how the conversation was going to go. I did not want to think carefully and guard every word that I spoke so I would not be judged.

Truth is that the only people who will turn away are the ones who cannot handle my truth because they cannot handle their own.

It was the denial, the hurt, the pain. I had to overcome that; it was taking me to a dark place.

I started standing in my truth. I became my safe place.

How could I be filled with joy if I am in denial of my real truths? How can I be honest in a relationship if I cannot be honest with myself? Transparency is the beginning of healing. Holding it all in did nothing but keep me filled with regret, hate, what-ifs, fear, and hurt. I had to talk about my thoughts to myself in the mirror.

I wrote them down in my journal.

I recorded my thoughts on my cell phone.

Transparency is freedom to be myself.

Transparency is a gift.

My transparency was not only a gift to me. My transparency became a gift to others as a safe space.

I WILL NEVER AGAIN BE
EMBARRASSED OR ASHAMED OF
THE PAIN AND STRUGGLE THAT I
ENDURED.

THERE IS SOMEONE OUT THERE
THAT MAY NEED TO HEAR MY
STORY.

5

MY SPACE OF LOVE

In this space of love, masks are not allowed. This is a place where I need to be vulnerable, this is the place where I know it is okay to cry, it is okay to let my thoughts out to be confronted by the truth. I cannot hide from myself in my space of love. In this space of love is where I came back to myself. This is where I brought back into existence my child-like faith and my playful spirit. This space calms me. Here, I am not anxious or scared.

I am humbly grateful for the absence of sound, for it was the absence of sound-silence introducing me and inviting me into my space of love.

This is where I learned that silence is not awkward. Silence is comforting. It let me collapse in its arms and held me with no judgment.

Silence was generous. It offered me the room to heal, ushering me to facing my truths, welcoming vulnerability. Engaging, and fully committing to my insecurities and weaknesses. I am living and thriving in this space of love I created for myself without the lies that will lead to detours in my healing. In this journey of healing, I have already taken many detours, so I refuse to tell myself lies. Lies should not navigate my journey, because then this space would not be of love it would be of lies.

THE ENERGY THAT FLOWS
THROUGH AND AROUND ME
CLEARS SPACE FOR ME TO GIVE
AND RECEIVE LOVE.

6

THE POWER OF RELEASE

I never gave up on trying to heal. I just never knew that healing is a lifelong course affording passage through my mind and manifesting into my soul in hopes of understanding my past, present, and future. Some of my thoughts destroyed me. In retrospect, I look back and I know that destruction of distracting thoughts was a part of the process of healing. I had to destroy to rebuild.

Most of the time I had no clue that I was healing. I thought I was trippin'. I now know that healing is a process and for me, it was painful, in the beginning teaching me patience. I not only had to have patience, but I also had to relearn what my granny told me about being gentle with myself along with many other cautionary conversations I did not listen to when she graced the earth.

In my case I believe the saying is true: "you cannot heal in the same environment you were hurt in." Some people can—it just so happens that I am one of the ones who cannot, and I had to be strong enough to realize that and release myself from the space that was harmful for me. Releasing is a part of the healing process, and as I released only sometimes my load was lightened.

Releasing has been powerful in deceptive ways. In the interest of releasing one thing I was holding onto, I subconsciously unblocked something else that I suppressed. Now unconsciously releasing something else that has come to the forefront of my healing all for the purpose of releasing that other thing. This was antagonizing and threatening to me. It brought up feelings of neglect, being unloved, not being good enough, and questioning my being. I was not sure what was happening, because when this happened, I felt unstable and frightened. My energy was running out.

This is where being gentle with myself played a huge part in my healing. I started taking mental health days. During these days I would cry and sit in the hurt, disappointment, and pain. Sometimes I would call the individuals involved with these thoughts and ask them "What happened?" I never did and probably never will get a direct answer. In my mind I knew it was generational. I felt if I made them name what happened, they too, would understand that it was generational and may want to stop it. I wanted to feel it, feel what made me so completely unhinged in the matter of a single thought. I would write about how it made me feel then, how it made me feel now, and what type of relationship that I had with the person who may have been involved in the memory. Most of all, I try to remember where I was mentally when it occurred. Then I was cool. I had to learn in the act of releasing that releasing is an action that I have the privilege of having, and not only having but utilizing as I see fit. An action that enabled me to heal. I had the power to release. So the thing that came up that I suppressed over the years that came to the forefront of my mind, in a manner that I was not expecting, telling me to deal with it now. I dealt with it and gave myself the authority to release it. That is how I started dealing in my power of release.

I RELEASE ALL THAT DOES NOT
SERVE ME TO MAKE SPACE FOR
ALL THAT I WAS PROMISED.

7

THE DRIVE HOME

How I hate going home driving down route 202. I see the blue and white Welcome to Delaware sign and my heart drops. I know I am almost home to a place where, no matter what, I am judged and made to feel shame leading me to living in fear and constantly apologizing for being me. I am either going to be alone in peace or there will be an overwhelming amount of drama there. I am never sure which one I will have. I wish I did not have these expectations, but this is my life and I never have misgivings about my life.

* * *

I view it as a stream where the water can be very still and very peaceful, but it can also be quite turbulent. My spirit, like a stream at times, flows through and sometimes against the winds of trouble, pain, hatred, fear, and temptation. When it happens, I hear the soft whisper of my granny telling me that I am saved by grace, mercy, and love—always have hope. I struggle with the soft whispers of her voice, "always have hope." I feel like holding onto hope has failed me. I feel as though I have been hoping my life away because of the trials I have failed. I do know when it feels like the stream is turning into a tidal wave it is a sign to stay strong, stay the course because it will be over soon. If I do not know where I am going, I just go with the flow of the stream. Wherever I end up is fine. I will get through it like always.

I NO LONGER GO WITH THE FLOW,
I DIRECT IT.

8

RECOVER ME

Some would say that by taking a job an hour and a half away in another state I was running from problems. This is true to a certain extent. As things go, I was running away to silence my mind so I could define my problems to overcome them. That hour and a half drive, twice a day, was a designated time for me to reflect on my life. I had to silence my mind and listen to me, listen, and to believe what I know to be true. For a long time, I gave people the permission to make up my mind for me. Now, it was time for me to make up my own mind and recover me.

When anyone asks me how I heal, I tell them: with a whole lot of patience and compassion toward myself, with the understanding that I am still in the process of healing and still forgiving me. There is no designated time frame for healing. It is ongoing for the duration of life. I cannot click my fingers and magically say I am healed. It is a tormenting, emotional journey where I was, and most times still am, shedding off layers of hurt, unleashing dysfunction, forgiving what I wanted to hate, relinquishing blame, extinguishing shame. Knowing that I am of my God and like God I am not, and will no longer be, of confusion. My soul struggled over a span of decades since I knew I wanted to live and not just survive. I did not want to just live to see another day. I wanted to live to be alive to thrive fully and whole-hardheartedly. I wanted to live a life full of joy. To do that, I had to recover who I was before I was told who I could not be, to transition into who I was becoming.

* * *

One day, on my hour and a half ride to work, I recollected accounts about how I was always inserting myself into the lives of others, coming up with solutions to their problems just so they would not feel as I did. In doing that, I was giving pieces of myself away and, at the same time, layering more insecurities and faults on top of the others I already accumulated. You know the saying "you cannot pour from an empty glass". Well, I was pouring the droplets I had left. I wanted whoever I was helping at that time to not ever feel worthless. As I was helping others, I was losing more of myself every second, or so I thought. My goal in life was to not let anyone I meet live a life surviving off hurt and pain or live their life in flip mode just to be happy or get by as I did at times. I did not have the courage or the confidence to believe in myself to heal myself. I thought I was lost, so I gave up on myself and placed my love and faith in fixing others. I was searching for a purpose, not in me. I was seeking it in others. I believed life would get better. I would be full of joy, never for myself, only for others. I could not win for myself, so I would help others win. I remembered how I would show up for others, because I thought I was too far gone to be healed.

I stayed building others up. "PUSH. Push Until Something Happens" they say. I was enjoying myself by pushing until something happened for someone else. I tried to help everyone—family, friends, associates—anyone I could, for I knew how it felt to be hurt and alone.

* * *

In collecting and examining my thoughts, I realized I had already started the healing process by helping others, and in helping others I was helping me. I was not worthless as my mind was trained in telling me, I was coming together slowly and surely. I thought about how I had a lot of wins for myself but downplayed my wins to others if I even mentioned them at all. I realized it was second nature for me to mention my losses and disappointments because, since I was pregnant at thirteen, it was implied that my life would be filled with losses and disappointments.

That was a lie.

What is done is done, but the past does not define the future. No one must believe it but me. In this belief I came to the realization that the trick was on me. I found joy in helping others. I was not losing myself as I thought, I was living in my purpose. Each time I helped someone I found peace in their joy. The joy we shared with each other.

I lacked the capacity to understand that I was already working in my purpose. I am here, helping, being present, effortlessly doing, placed here in the universe to share my wins, my gifts, extending all that I was given in grace with grace. Like others had done for me. I was paying it forward, paving a way for others.

As I write this, I know that I did not ever have to struggle. I was afraid to live in abundance because my mind was programmed by the words that were said to me. I really believed I was not worthy.

I AM WORTHY.

9

SHIFTING IN HIV

There was an unfortunate turn of events that changed my life again. I had lost my job, thanks to my speaking up as usual. I decided and stood firm on what came from my mouth and the universe strategically placed me in a place my soul was yearning for. I was an administrator of two HIV studies. As the participants waited to be seen, I would talk to them about how their week was going. They told me not only how their week was going, but also how they contracted HIV/AIDS. If they were not living with HIV/AIDS, they told me about the risky behaviors they indulged in.

These were honest conversations that opened my heart to individuals that, if I just walked by them on the streets, I would have made up stories in my mind based on how they looked, how they dressed, the flamboyant flick of their wrists, the exaggerated outfits that I wished I had the confidence to wear. Some of these conversations not only upset me, but they also filled me with so much anger I wanted to strangle someone for taking advantage of these individuals. Some were mentally challenged, others had low confidence, others were extremely easy to fall into the trap of a sexual predator because, like me, they wished to find love. It hurt me more than I cared to admit. I empathized with every one of them. I wanted to hold them and tell them it was okay or just shake them, letting them know they were being used and abused and this is not what love is.

I stayed quiet, not exposing my true feelings as I remained a listening ear. That listening ear taught me that sometimes a person may have to hear themselves say something out loud to understand the true meaning of what is happening to them. Sometimes the person does not understand the veracity of what is going on with them because they were born into chaos. That chaos shaped their lives and that is why they made decisions as I did. It was normal to them as it was to me, considering chaos was all they knew. They knew nothing about trauma or did not even think about it. I used to judge and say no one is blind. They feel what is being done to them, they know it is a problem and that the attention, bad or good, is attention that they may have lacked once upon a time.

That is not the case every time. We all believe in love. We all believe in faith and we all believe in hope, and it is those three things that blind us from seeing the truth in others and that binds us to those people who are hurting us. We are told to have faith in all things. Every decision I ever went into was with blind faith. They did not turn out all bad either. That is why I would leave the patients with an affirmation. Usually, it was whatever I posted on social media that morning. "I AM worthy." Something as easy as that. Left them walking away with that final thought. They are worthy of whatever their hearts desire.

* * *

Two years later, I was asked to be a research interviewer on an intervention project examining a process using wraparound services for substance users living with HIV. I interviewed individuals while they were inpatients in the hospital. Some of these interviews lasted up to six hours in a hospital room, and some went on for two to three days, depending on the person.

This is where another shift happened in me. A shift that I was not scared of once I felt comfortable maneuvering in it. It was something I felt in my spirit. My life changed drastically when I started working with people living with HIV. I was somehow helping them get and stay in care by being that listening ear and listening to their stories. A funny thing happened. I ended up getting the care I needed, staying in care, and receiving healing. I was becoming healthy, full of joy, and on my way to whole. What a turnaround. They pushed me deeper into my journey of healing without even knowing it. Just surviving, and living a life—one life, not two—and being full of joy. Because of these individuals, I showed up and sometimes out for them within the boundaries of the hospital rules and the Internal Review Boards' regulations. I learned that the participants had a moment of freedom when I was in their presence. In that freedom I discovered what I was doing to deter me from being filled with joy. I had been letting my family control my freedom instead of telling them to go suck an egg. The freedom that these participants shared through their stories—about them continuing to participate in activities, chasing a high they know they will never be able to feel again, knowing they will never relive that moment they are trying desperately to relive—that moment is the common denominator of all my conversations. There was no question that asked, "How did you feel the first time you got high?" Yet the participants offered this information. It was the best moment they ever had in their life and they wanted to share it. I cannot even begin to describe the feelings they felt once they reached that high in this book. I can only write about the joy in their smiles as they spoke about the high or the sadness I see in their eyes when they talk about not having the feeling they had in the moment of their first hit. As they told their stories, I heard hope in their voices. I took the perking up and smiling as promise in their eyes. Their truths opened my world, and what they poured into me changed my life forever.

No matter what anyone says, no two stories are alike. There may be similarities only. Everyone has a different perspective about the story they are sharing. It is my duty to listen without judgment. Non-judgement and compassion lead to real change, as does not putting an end time on anything, especially recovery or healing, in my case. The participants trusted me with their secrets, their deep thoughts, their whys, and why nots. Their answers to my behavioral assessment questions were their opening to forgiving themselves and looking deeper into themselves. Realizing they were more than someone who uses drugs. They were someone's mom, dad, aunt, uncle, friend, employee. And not only that. They were themselves, unique, made different in the eyes of our creator to make mistakes. They were human beings capable of being cared about and caring about others. I realized that the compassion, non-judgment, and tough love that I gave them were what I had been yearning to receive my whole life. That compassion, non-judgment, and tough love from my family. I wanted a moment of freedom from my family that I was able to secure on behalf of the participants. Thanks to them, I realized that many moments have passed, and by surviving in a cage I built to secure me, I have missed out on so many moments of enjoyment. I understood I was waiting hopelessly for moments of enjoyment with my family that I once had and will not receive again. I let the joy escape me at each turn, wallowing in self-pity, placing myself in the cage I built around myself . . . I could not break free. I could not move on from being trapped in a moment.

Although it looked as if I were moving forward, I was mentally stuck. I could move forward, but I was simply scared of what my family would think of me. No, I did not use drugs, no I did not have HIV. However, like these participants, I suffered from trauma. I will never forget the first person I interviewed. So many obstacles ran through my mind. We calculated that the assessment I would administer would take approximately ninety minutes.

* * *

I had not spent more than fifteen minutes in a hospital room since my son was released from the hospital after suffering from a coma. When I went into hospital rooms after my son's incident, I would hyperventilate and have heart palpitations. I would replay the events moment by moment, my son arriving at the hospital and me beating the ambulance to the ER. Watching them arrive to take my son into a room and witnessing my son's body jump up off the stretcher, landing perfectly back on the stretcher to go into a coma. I thought he jumped because he heard my voice, but the nurses said it was from shock. Me sitting in his room, calm as I have ever been in my life, waiting for my God to make his next move. I would rejoice in that moment when he came out of his coma months later. Recalling that the first time I left him alone, he came out of his coma, so now I am not rejoicing. I am mad at myself for leaving him in the hospital to move my belongings into my granny's home. Now I think that I should have just hired Dwayne to move everything out of my apartment to the house on his own.

* * *

Hospital rooms and Emergency rooms were a trigger that placed me on a real emotional rollercoaster. I took this position despite all that. So yes, during the first interview of my first person, I froze. I stood still and teared up as soon as I walked through the door of the hospital room. I put on my armor of confidence and politely introduced myself to the patient I was hoping would become a participant. This was challenging and I had to do it. The participant welcomed me . . . thank goodness, he made it easy. When I walked into the hospital room there came a rollercoaster of all kinds of emotions in sixty seconds. That armor mysteriously fell off and I was vulnerable. Then I smiled, as this person looked familiar, like someone I used to know.

He was interested in the study and that is when I said, "There is a disclaimer I need you to hear." He looked at me. I said what I would go on to say to almost two hundred individuals in the next two years. "I am going to be all up in your business, up close and personal. Do not lie, because I will know, and be honest. That way, I can help you and others that would benefit from you taking part in this study." That opening line, "being all up in my binezz" was a hit, they still talk about that today.

I wanted them to know these questions were extremely sensitive, so I did not want them to be embarrassed by their answers. There is no shame in the choices they made, because in that time it made them feel good. There was no reason to be ashamed. I would tell them "This is life, and in life we make good and bad decisions. Things happen. So answering the questions honestly may not directly benefit you right now, it may benefit people in the future."

I did not know it then, but I was the person it would benefit in the future. Who knew! Not only that, but some participants benefited directly in those moments of assessment because they were releasing what they were holding on to for so long.

Life is certainly amazing. It is. You just must sit still, be present, and listen. Change the trajectory of your comfort level. I did. I accepted the position knowing I hated hospitals. That they made me cry contributing to me living moments in the past where I was helpless. I accepted the position knowing I am an introvert. I had no idea why I accepted the position since it was a paralegal job waiting for me downtown. I thought I wanted it. I felt I was now partial to this cause (HIV).

* * *

We all make mistakes. I felt as if I could be these people. I could have smoked cocaine or marijuana when I was young if someone had not told me to roll my own blunt. I could have chosen to use drugs as a vice instead of flipping. I could have joined in at Mattie's with the corporate bigwigs who sniffed cocaine. I chose not to, although I could have. I could have contracted HIV from having risky sex with people. I did not though. We have choices, we take chances, and they change us in all types of ways. So yes, instead of asking why or how could you, I asked what led you to these choices or how did you get to the place you are at today. These are all the questions I had to ask myself. It was hard because, as I was asking the participants the questions, I was answering them in my head for myself.

Taking the time to understand the reasoning behind the choices we make is a skill that helped me in healing. In this position I made the participants confront their life, they had to stop a minute, sober up. They had to not only live in the present and become aware of how they came to be in the hospital this time, with me working on this study they also had to confront the trauma within them.

What HIV has taught me is that being vulnerable can be a strength if acknowledged. When you are being vulnerable, you are healing from the inside out. Being vulnerable reminded me of getting my wisdom teeth pulled. The anxiety I felt, the imagined pain I endured during the process, and then the real pain I underwent during the healing process. Now I understand being vulnerable is a strength I was once afraid of. Being vulnerable shows a sense of pride for what I have been through and strength on the road to healing. Exposing myself and standing in my truth offers a freedom that allows me to go out into the world saying, "take me as I AM." Being vulnerable only chases away the people who are scared to stand in their truth.

As I write this, the word *trauma* is written all over. Then the question I ask myself is how we deal with the trauma of not only ourselves but also the people we encounter. How do we handle them? As they say, "Everyone we come across is going through something or has been through something."

We all go through pain, hurt, grief, some type of trauma, and that's life. It is how we deal with the trauma that defines us. How do we mask the pain? Do we claim strength to elude the reality, or do we do the work by talking and feeling through it? Doing the work is arduous and, at times, even distressful. Yet it allowed me to come to an understanding of my trauma, exploring the depths of my thoughts as I flourish through the process, allowing myself passage to my new reality.

I AM DIVING DEEP INTO ME AND
DOING THE WORK NEEDED FOR
ME TO BECOME THE BEST
VERSION OF ME.

10

LOYALTY TO HEALING

I must avoid it: Drama. It creates a ball of negative energy that, if I give it attention, will create a fire that I cannot put out. What a waste of energy. I have wasted a considerable amount of energy already trying to recover from the past. I should avoid drama, and not only avoid drama but no longer create it in the name of unresolved trauma. Each moment I have is precious and I will be using it wisely. I cannot participate in events that do not serve me. My coping mechanism is my loyalty to healing.

As I am healing, I realized that friends and family do matter, but it is not my priority for me to show up for them. If I do show up, I show up in a way that is healthy for me. It may not be what they want, but loyalty to healing is real. I cannot worry about what it looks like if I do not show up or worry about what people will have to say. My healing is first and foremost, and setbacks are real. My healing resides in a safe place, and I must protect it no matter what that looks like and how it may come across. In being loyal to my healing process, I am conscious about who I spend time with and the conversations I have.

Excuse me while I heal.

I AIN'T TRIPPIN'...I AM HEALING.

11

I DO NOT WANT TO BE STRONG

My ego was once a strong wrestling partner of mine, especially when it came to me feeling vulnerable and threatened. I wanted, needed to be strong. Sometimes being strong can be a facade and burying myself in the facade of being strong did not give me space to heal, to be vulnerable, to let go. The facade of being strong caused suffering and kept me isolated. Being strong wore me down. I was exhausted. I had to let go. I accepted vulnerability, creating room to breathe, to think, to let go, and making room for more love, more compassion, more positive thoughts. Understanding it is okay to let it all go, reset, rest, and restore.

I do not want to be strong; I want to let it out. I want to pray out loud about it, asking for help. I want to let my ego go. I do not want to act strong to tolerate pain. I do not pride myself on tolerating a great deal of pain and suffering. I do not want to tolerate pain. I want to move on and learn from it. I want to focus on my personal journey in my healing. I want meaningful development. I do not want to be strong. In being strong, I let my ego shove my safety nets to the side. I gave my ego full reign since I had to keep up my facade. There were a lot of things I could not handle. I acted as if I had life under control. I was scared to ask for help for fear of someone saying "I told you so" or using the help they would give me against me.

A safety net is there to protect me from injuring myself and to make sure I have a soft landing to lower the risk of damage to myself. Those nets are there for a reason. They have a purpose. I had to learn to utilize the ones I had. I could no longer be apprehensive in asking for help. I had to lean on the ones who never left my side, who would check on me. I had to lose the facade of being strong and welcome my safety nets.

BEING STRONG IS OVERRATED, MENTALLY EXHAUSTING AND ISOLATING.

12

REMAINING CONTINUALLY UNCHANGED

My uncle reminded me of my poppy. Loving, serious men of not many words. They both had the same chuckle where the corners of their mouth would rise, their teeth would show, and a little chuckle would come out before quickly they both would go back to their serious self. Honestly, I do not remember seeing them together, but my uncle and poppy reminded me so much of each other in the way they cared for me. When my uncle would call home from prison I would stand on the tip of my toes and jump up and down until I was offered the phone. My voice calmed. I would act as if I were not excited and say, "Whatcha doing Uncle David?" He would talk, but then cut me off and say to put mom back on the phone. I would give her the phone, smiling away. I loved to talk to him because, unlike my poppy, his tone never changed. Like my granny, he was always calm. I loved going to see him in prison. He was always the same, he was kind to the prison guards just like he was kind to me, and I never heard him complain about prison during our visits. I remember our visits being fun. It was like a family reunion, sitting, talking, eating, and laughing, and I always complained and cried when time was up. I never wanted to leave because I felt safe with him. He was a comfort to me. His voice alone always placed me in a state of peace. He did not care that I was silly and rambunctious and all over the place.

* * *

I was so excited when he was released and even more excited when I heard he was staying at my granny's with me. He was strict. Not mean but strict. I could never get away with anything with him. I could talk anyone out of anything, or they just gave me my way because I was the baby, but either way it did not matter. Correcting me, he would always lead with "it's for your own good" just like my poppy. I listened to him because when he said that I believed him. He never gave me any reason to doubt him. For the short time he stayed with us my routine stayed the same every morning. Upon waking, I would stand in the hallway and debate on waking up my uncle. His door was always closed and even though he slept on the bottom bunk head closest to the door he would act like he did not hear me making noise by sliding things under his door. I would just go and softly tap on his door so granny would not hear me. It never worked. Then I would knock on the door until he said "huh" and I would say "whatcha doing Uncle David." He would say "Good morning, I was sleep." I would smile and say okay and run up the hallway, slapping my bare feet against the floor as loud as I could to make sure he was getting up. As it occurred one day, he did not answer his door at all, so I opened the door, and there was a woman with him in his bed. I knew what that meant for my uncle. I was so upset. Not for long though because her family was so welcoming and brought so much joy to me and my granny. Her family was what my granny and I were missing. My granny was happy and so was I. During summers I would stay at their house, and I loved it. Through the year we would have parties at my granny's for my uncle and his girlfriend and her family. Sometimes in the backyard and sometimes in our small house. We would have games for me and the other kids, music, everyone talking and, of course, I was always the center of attention. They did not mind me talking so much. To me it reminded me of the family reunions at the prison. I was in my glory.

* * *

I remember on my uncle's wedding day I was running around in a blue dress, and my uncle seemed off. Very off. It set off concern in me. I became scared, and in that little bit of time I felt my heart breaking. I felt I was going to lose my uncle. I could no longer run around in that big yard, and I wanted to go and cry because all I was thinking was that someone else was going to change on me. So many scenarios went through my mind. Then he noticed me, and he came and talked to me. It was a very brief conversation, with the same calming tone he always had. Everything was fine and he remained the same. That moment sticks with me, because in my little decade of life he, like my granny and dad, he was the only person who remained continually unchanged.

* * *

Years later, when I became pregnant, he did not look at me any different. He was still comforting, and I viewed him as my safe place. He never gave up on me. He always welcomed my over-the-top personality and my high-pitched voice. His voice still makes me feel safe. The conversations are still brief. They go like:

"Whatcha doing Uncle David?"

"Ohhhh, watching TV."

"I didn't want nothing just to see what you were doing."

"Ok, I talk to you later."

"Ok."

THE PERSON MY UNCLE HAS CONTINUED TO BE FOR ME, I PRAY I CAN BE THAT PERSON FOR SOMEONE.

13

SELF FORGIVENESS

I felt sad because I had to prove my worth.

I was not good enough, but I was.

I forgive myself for judging myself as worthless.

I am actively engaged in my present moment holding for all things in loving kindness.

I acknowledge myself for the love I give.

I appreciate that I am forgiving and capable of accepting forgiveness.

I forgive myself for holding on to ideas, people and places that never served me.

I am physically strong, mentally focused, supported, and spiritually aware of my divinity.

I forgive myself for continuously trying to prove to myself and others that there is such a thing as unconditional love. I forgive myself because I learned from a place of conditional love. I let myself get hurt trying to prove there is such a thing as unconditional love.

I forgive myself for believing in who they said I was and not believing in who *I am*. I forgive myself for being hard on myself for the mistakes I made. I acknowledge I am human and a part of being human is making mistakes. I remember I am better today than I was yesterday, and tomorrow I will be better than I am today. And if for some reason I may not feel better I will acknowledge my feelings and move on in forgiveness.

My aunt always reminds me that the most wonderful things in life come after we forgive.

FORGIVING MYSELF IS A FORM OF
SELF-LOVE.

14

I FORGAVE TO LET GO

When you forgive, you are letting go of the anger that may be keeping you from succeeding. Forgiveness is a quality that most of us lack for our own reasons. People say forgive and pray for our enemies. I understood and thought I had done just that, but my actions and thoughts implied otherwise. So, one day when I was saying my prayers, I realized I prayed for someone who I thought I had forgiven. It was not until that night I prayed that all was really forgiven. Once you forgive a person or situation, they no longer have power over you. Forgiveness shows strength. It shows that you are the bigger person. No, you will not forget, but when you remember the event or person you will not be livid. You will be reminded of how you let it go and moved on with grace.

If you do not practice forgiveness, you might be the one who pays most dearly. By embracing forgiveness, you can also embrace peace, hope, gratitude, and joy. Consider how forgiveness can lead you down the path of physical, emotional, and spiritual wellbeing.

Forgiveness is a decision to let go of resentment and thoughts of pain. Forgiveness can even lead to feelings of understanding, empathy, and compassion for the one who hurt you.

For me, forgiveness is another form of releasing, I had to stop holding on and let it go.

I FORGIVE BECAUSE I HAVE BEEN FORGIVEN.

15

TOOLS OF FEAR

Avoidance and indirectness were words that propped themselves up in the back of my mind each time I had to confront a problem. Early in my journey, I felt that these words would surface because they were obstacles to my growth and healing, and I needed to identify the reason behind why I enlisted them so much to come to my aid. I had to stop avoiding unwanted conversations because they were an opportunity for growth. A lesson in my wrongs. A chance to acknowledge and/or correct them to move forward. I used avoidance as a tool so I would not have to deal with an issue in hopes of the person never bringing it up again. I used indirectness as a tool of deceit, speaking without being direct about the matter I was speaking of, saying what I wanted without the other person knowing how I really felt in hopes of getting my way. I eagerly used avoidance and indirectness as tools to aid in my resistance to growth. Yet I felt resentment toward myself each time I used them, replaying the situations repeatedly in my head. It was exhausting. It was mentally taking a toll on me.

* * *

I gave up on avoidance and indirectness for identifying and admitting so I could grow. Avoidance and indirectness were tools I enlisted when I was walking in fear, not living in my authenticity.

48

Once I identified those obstacles and admitted they were, in fact, obstacles, I started winning in life. I stopped avoiding them and started using them as tools to aid in my healing and growth. Identifying meant I had to acknowledge what was holding me back. Acknowledging that something is holding me back was admitting my resistance to moving forward, condemning myself to a state of mediocrity, coming up with excuse after excuse.

Once I surrendered to those things, the maturing process began, enabling me to step out of my comfort zone. I no longer walk in fear and those tools—avoidance and indirectness—are no longer being utilized in my life.

LIFE WITHOUT A DOUBT WILL
BRING OBSTACLES,
UNCOMFORTABLE SITUATIONS,
DISAPPOINTMENTS,PAIN, AND
HURTS.

HOWEVER, WHAT I CHOOSE TO DO
IN THOSE SITUATIONS IS UP TO
ME.

16

ALONE WAS COOL, AROUND PEOPLE I WAS LONELY

I was never afraid of being alone because most of the time when I was alone, I would write or read or just sit there and think. Alone in silence I thrived. Alone is where I acquired an understanding of myself. Alone, I was safe, with no one to ridicule me, no one comparing themselves to something they heard or thought about me. No one to worry about turning on me and no one for me to take on their feelings, their attitude, or whatever drama they were carrying. Alone was safe and in silence, I was at peace.

When I was surrounded by people is when I felt most lonely. I did not know how to interact with people as myself. I always felt awkward around people, as if I did not fit in. Although, if you knew me, you would have no clue that I became weird around people. It was a safety issue (I think). It may still exists at times. Isolating myself around people was a way to protect me. I wanted to gain a better understanding of myself and my interaction with others. At this point in my life, my interactions with people were based on the premise of not being good enough. In discussions, I would either lash out or over-explain myself and most of the time neither was warranted. I was taking everything personal. I was tired of wearing a mask and tired of being lonely and isolating myself away from people when I was around them. I had to change that.

One indulgence I had was taking myself out on dinner and movie dates. To help me stop feeling so lonely in groups of people, I started going to restaurants that held happy hour in their bar areas. To develop confidence, I would introduce myself to the bartender and the patrons. It was hard at first, but I was testing my confidence and how I could manage being in a room full of people without putting on my invisible mask and conforming to what I felt they wanted. I had my mind made up and I was going to do this. I love talking.

At first it was so much effort but then it became effortless. Enjoying the company of others as myself and gaining confidence all in one. It felt good. I learned that most people are welcoming and do not require anything but good conversation.

MY INTERACTIONS WITH PEOPLE ARE WITH AN OPEN MIND THAT IS FREE OF BAGGAGE.

17

I WORE A MASK

A mask is a manner of expression that hides one's true character or feelings.

I wore a mask and when wearing one I tripped a lot and felt awkward, not myself, and insecure.

When I wore the mask, I was not only hiding who I was but the gifts and talents I was given.

I had to take the mask off to be my true self so I could cultivate and embrace the gifts and talents I was given. I had to begin to trust and think of myself as a queen, with the plans, hopes, dreams, purpose, and destiny I was blessed with. I could not let my surroundings define how I perceived myself.

I wore a mask to hide my true character.

The mask damaged me.

The mask suppressed who I was and who I was becoming.

I wore the mask to satisfy others.

I hid who I was from my family and gave them what they expected of me.

I hid my gifts and talents since, when I spoke of them, I was ridiculed and talked about.

I wore the mask because I wanted to be a part of something.

Maybe I wore the mask for protection since once I removed the mask, I went to battle . . . mentally with myself and physically with others. More than once, more than twice, more than three times.

* * *

I became tired so I took the mask off and lived my life in joy.

Now I come as I am.

Wherever I go and in whatever I do, I AM ME.

I come as I AM.

No need for a mask or even to solely identify only as someone's child, parent, significant other, the position I may hold, or my background. Those things are just a small part of me. They all played a part in becoming me. But there is more to me. I am kind, gentle, intelligent, a go-getter, corny, forgiving, loving, protective, weird, talkative, confident, and I can go on and on. All these things together are what makes me thrive because I come as I am, letting the naysayers see the confidence in my walk, the aspiration in my eyes, and the passion in my speech. I am becoming the woman I was born to be, walking shoulder to shoulder with the thirteen-year-old me, telling her, "It's not your fault." Walking hand in hand with the six-year-old me, thanking her for not letting go of joy.

I WILL NEVER SUPPRESS MYSELF
TO SATISFY ANYONE ELSE.

EVER.

18

TEN MONTHS

At thirteen I had sexual intercourse.

During sexual intercourse, I became with child.

I told no one.

I was ashamed.

When my stomach began to intensify to a rounding shape, I said it was a tumor and I needed surgery.

I was ashamed.

In May, the Friday before Memorial Day weekend, Coach Swatley called my mother and informed her I could not run track anymore because I was with child.

The next couple of days were a blur.

I remember my bed and my clothes being thrown out in the front yard of my granny's house.

Quickly my granny pushed me out the back door and I knew to jump in her car. She drove me in town to my great-grandmom's (her mother's) house. She said I could not go home until she said it was safe.

The next week my mother was at my middle school arguing with my counselor to keep me in school the last two weeks. I was on the school bus the next day.

That next month I was beaten down and kicked multiple times in the stomach for being a spoiled brat and how my unborn baby was already a spoiled brat.

I went to the emergency room and the doctor stated that me and my baby would be fine.

My granny did not take me home to her house, she took me home to my mother's house she said to keep me safe.

A month later, on what was supposed to be my first day of high school, I was sitting in the living room waiting on my mom as she finished the morning dishes to take me to school to get my assignments. I felt something, forgetting all about what my visiting nurse explained to me, I said, "Mom, I just peed myself. I'm sorry, it just came." This huge smile came across her face and she started screaming as she called my granny, still screaming, then called my dad, still screaming. Then she called my doctor, not screaming anymore but code-switching to her professional authoritative, sweet white woman voice. By that time, I had heard her say and I remembered what the visiting nurse tried to prepare me for.

My water broke.

In the hospital, I remember feeling something vibrating on my stomach. Maybe it was even ticklish accompanied by a grinding sound.

I remember someone saying he swallowed fluid. I saw a glimpse of him. He was enormous. I could not hold him because I felt loopy.

I did not want to hold him anyway after I heard somebody say he swallowed fluid.

Already I started not protecting my baby.

I was so upset.

I cried.

He had to be placed on a ventilator.

My granny had never left my side.

People kept asking for a name for my baby.

For nine months when I talked to my stomach, I called the fetus growing inside "My baby." I never thought of a name. For the whole nine months, I just thought about how I would protect my baby. I prayed over my baby. But never by name, just My baby.

All my Barbies had names.

All my Cabbage Patch kids had names.

All my characters I wrote about had names.

Why, in TEN months, did I not name my real baby?

My granny started knitting, nothing entertaining was on television, so I opened and reached in the nightstand next to the hospital bed and pulled the Bible out and read the first chapter of Timothy then on to the second chapter.

[2]To Timothy, *my* dearly beloved son: Grace, mercy, *and* peace, from God the Father and Christ Jesus our Lord.

[3]I thank God, whom I serve from *my* forefathers with pure conscience, that without ceasing I have remembrance of thee in my prayers night and day; [4]Greatly desiring to see thee, being mindful of thy tears, that I may be filled with joy; [5]When I call to remembrance the unfeigned faith that is in thee, which dwelt first in thy grandmother Lois, and thy mother Eunice; and I am persuaded that in thee also.

[6]Wherefore I put thee in remembrance that thou stir up the gift of God, which is in thee by the putting on of my hands.[7]For God hath not given us the spirit of fear; but of power, and of love, and of a sound mind.[1]

I had the widest grin. I could not stop grinning. I recall being so excited. Talking ten miles per hour I blurted out, "Granny, OH EM Gee, Timothy! Only because I long to see him and he brings me joy and fills me with faith that I will be okay . . . the faith you and great-grandmom keep telling me to hold on to. And it is perfect right. You won't give up on us right."

The nurse rolled my baby into my room, and I held him. He was huge. I cried tears of joy.

I told the nurse he would be Timothy.

I came to be a mom at fourteen.

LOVE COVERED ME THROUGH THE
PURIFICATION OF FIRE.

19

MOTHER OF A
FATHERLESS CHILD

I said many times before that I will never know how it is to be a fatherless child. I only know what it is to struggle to raise a fatherless child. Not only to raise a fatherless child, but a fatherless child who is a boy who craves the attention of a father, a dad, a man just to call him Pop. Honestly, it is hard as hell, as it goes, whatever the circumstance I compete with the idea of what that child wants in a father, with the child not paying attention to what, as a mother, I have sacrificed for that child's happiness. That child looks at other father/son relationships and wonders why he will never have that relationship that he desires. Inciting feelings of confusion, hostility, uncertainty, and more emotions that one cannot handle. This leads into a life of constantly asking his self, "Why am I not good enough?" Regardless of whether I tell him he is good enough and overcompensates on behalf of the father, there will be these thoughts in the back of his mind saying he is not. Already being born into this cruel world to a fourteen-year-old mom who plays with Barbies, who was insecure and abused. This child has been already labeled by society and not only by society. This child has been labeled by the person who planted him as a seed when he said, "that's not my baby!" A phrase coined by men who do not want to take responsibility for raising a child and think of it as a burden. Born into this world of a teenage mom, no father, and no hope to live a productive life in a society that already has placed a target on his back. Life is hard enough being raised by an abused single teenage mother who was beaten and kicked in the stomach by her uncle during the pregnancy, learning to protect her seed by any means necessary since he became a seed. I overwhelmed my child with love and protection and did and will still do everything in my will to protect him from this cold society and the woes that he will encounter in this life. My lesson was not to depend on anyone, and if the father said he would do something or give him something, that was extra. Standards were a little high for Timmy since it was important to me to be versatile for him so that he could understand this world and be empowered to make not only positive, alternatively confident life choices, but be sure of who he is and the power he holds as a child whose mother overcame a lot. I wanted him to know that there may be obstacles, and the only thing that can stop him from becoming what he wanted was him. It was not enough that I wanted those things for him. He wanted his father to want that for him as well.

I will never know how it feels to be a leading pitcher for the Dunleith Originals. When all the people who lived on the street you grew up on show up to root for him, the baseball star, his grandpop, and whoever he brought with him, and everyone else that showed up to support the child. And then the father rides by in a tricked-out car and all you hear is base from his kicker. He parks over at the park and does not come to the baseball field which is less than three hundred feet away to see his seed strike the opposing team out. I will never know how that feels because there was not one time my dad was not on the sideline rooting for me. I just know how, as the mother, it gave me feelings of regret given at thirteen I let a nineteen-year-old boy pick me to be the mother of his fatherless child. I had no regrets, as I had no control over the situation, and I could not make it better. I do not regret how my childhood friends taught him how to say his father's name, saying it was important for him to know. And it was so cute when he said it, thanks to him having a lisp and sounded so adorable when he spoke. My friends and I were praying and wishing that this fatherless child would not remain fatherless.

He remained that way for a time.

* * *

The father came around, however, with conditions and for various reasons, usually about once or twice a year if that. Even so, the child remained fatherless with me preparing myself for the child's anger and hostility that would be misdirected toward me turning into a lifetime of hurt. I could not protect him from false hope and broken promises that ultimately turned into hopelessness and doubt equaling a broken heart. Even though I said, "the father came around," he still was absent.

* * *

I will never know how it feels to see my father be a father to others who are not his. And when the child sees the father, it is as if he is looking into a mirror. I will never know how that feels. I can not even begin to imagine. I just know how it feels to be the mother of one. Sometimes it is not a good feeling. Especially when that child hurts because of these very reasons. I cannot do or say anything to make it better.

That child's hurt turns into a mother's hate. When you are struggling mentally to raise a boy, the only thing you should have room in your heart for is love, comfort, and protection. My protection for my seed goes without saying. I started protecting my seed once he formed in my womb. I never told anyone I was pregnant to protect him from that procedure that people get. Once it was known I was six months along. That procedure was not happening that far along, I knew that! I tried to protect him from my abusers, as they could not get to him physically, although they were able to get to him mentally. I wanted to protect him from his father yet that was out of the question since there will remain hope that the father stays in his life and keeps his word. It was hard, it was a struggle. Still, it would be okay. I passionately believe that one day he will be a constant in the child's life and the false hope will no longer be false and all the promises made will be kept.

* * *

What I learned is that a father, dad, pop has a responsibility to nurture and love their seed so they can grow and become successful. They have the responsibility to offer encouragement, love, and understanding to strengthen them. A father may make mistakes, yet he recognizes them and takes responsibility for them, setting a premise for that child. I believe when that child hears that father's voice, that voice should arouse a feeling of solace signaling to that child that everything will be okay, just from the sound of that voice.

* * *

The hardest part of my life was being a mom. Of course, I was not ready. Nevertheless, I wanted to try. God allowed me to be this vessel and carry him full term and bring him into this world regardless of the consequences. I am thankful my vessel and my mind was strong enough to endure not only the physical pain but also the mental abuse I went through to bring him into this world. Honestly, I knew it was hard being a mom, yet I was young and naïve and believed that love, hope, and faith would not only lead the way but conquer all.

I TRIED MY BEST AND THAT IS ALL I COULD DO-MY BEST.

20

SHE WILL BE FINE I WILL BE BETTER

I was in the psychiatrist office just talking away as I usually do and then I quieted down for a moment, dwelling in my space, letting go of my ego, and reflecting on the past weekend and the visit with my mom and the psychiatrist asks me, "How do you feel about what happened this past weekend with your mom?" Right then, as Oprah says, I had an "AHA moment" and I said to my psychiatrist, "She will be fine, and I will be better." Those breakthrough moments are the ones that come from the most difficult situations. I had to say "No" to myself so I could say "Yes" to living my best life.

* * *

Why will I be better? First, I took my ego out of the situation. This was not about me and never has been. This was not even about me being a teenage mom at fourteen. How she treats me has never been about me. I will be better because I now know that I must accept that I will never get an apology for the things that were done to me because that is the way she was raised. I have shown her grace, forgiven her, and wished her well. I will be better because, when I think of her, my eyes will always dance with joy. I know I will love her immensely for being that vessel for me and delivering me into this world. I will be better because I appreciate the good times we shared, appreciate the beauty she has given me, I appreciate the man she chose to be my dad, I appreciate the nose she bestowed upon me (it is perfect) and I appreciate the sense of style she gave me. I appreciate her placing my highly spirited self in multiple dance classes so I could explore and express my feelings through dance. Also, I appreciate my mother for giving permission to my granny to start me in counseling at such a young age. It shows she tried. I appreciate her showing me how to fight for love, how to love unconditionally, and how to forgive and be forgiven without acknowledgment. I also appreciate how she fought for me on multiple occasions when she would state, "That's my f*cking daughter." I am grateful to her for pushing me to be better than the expectations she had for me. I am thankful to her for teaching me how to endure the pain that I would endure through my life. She taught me how to love my body, mind, and spirit—the whole package. Sometimes we learn the opposite of what we are shown. From my mother, I learned that doing a great job at work is not fueled by working hard, it is fueled by patience, paying attention to detail, and understanding that we can only do our best. (I wish she believed that I was only doing my best as a child). The most important lesson I gained from how I was treated by her was to have compassion and empathy for not only myself but for others as well. And to not only feel my emotions, but to also identify, examine, and reflect upon them so that I could understand my reaction or non-reaction to them. I had to sit in my emotions so I could understand them, to understand the "why" in all of this. Again, as I wrote above sometimes, we learn the opposite of what we are shown. Now, several decades later, I know it is not my "why" to understand, figure out, or apologize for. I just needed to move on and stop yearning and hoping for the idea of the love I have of a mother/daughter relationship. It is my mom's "why" and hers alone to deal with it as she pleases. I honor that as I honor me by not allowing myself to be a physical and mental punching bag for whatever her "why" is.

* * *

Writing this is hard. As I write, I heal and as I heal the more, I understand I romanticized the idea of a mother/daughter relationship that I will never get. My idea has died and given birth to actual new beginnings for me, and all has been forgiven. Why I proclaim actual new beginnings for me, is because it has been hoping that kept me going. In this situation, the idea of *hope* was what kept me from accepting the reality of the present and the future. How many new beginnings can one person have with another person that wants nothing to do with them? I would say every time that this is going to be a new beginning for my mom and me. Every time I would plan to see her, I would say we are going to have a new beginning and she will love me. It never happened, but I never gave up because I had hope. Who gives up on fighting for the love of their mom? I did not, until now. I prayed and rehearsed, I conversed with people about what I should do, I shopped for her before every new beginning I thought would happen with my mom. Yet again there was the same ending with me being ridiculed and feeling threatened. The more you repeat the choices you make the worse it gets. I just wanted her to know me and that I was able to get out of that imaginary box. I am bigger and have become better than the expectation she had of me. I wanted her to be proud of me. She did not have to say it, just apply it in her actions. Just smile, laugh, hug me, kiss me on the cheek.

* * *

There was a lot of pain that I endured by my mom, and I welcomed it. The beatings were excruciating. I welcomed them because I thought the pain that my mother was feeling would be transferred to me every time she hit me. I wanted to take her pain away so that she could be happy. I wanted her not to feel the pain of whatever she was going through that made her want to hurt me so badly. It was the love I yearned for. It was the relationship I tried so hard to forge, and the hope of us that kept me enduring the pain. Pain in its form of physical or mental capacity is the universal human denominator we all share. We empathize with each other's pain. At my young age I romanticized the pain. I not only worshipped the person who inflicted it, but I also loved that person more than me. It was not hard because I wanted my mom to be better. I am not sure if I was being brave or a coward. At ten years old, who knows really? I thought it was a sign of bravery. Sometimes I did not want to go home with her. Then I would cry to stay at my grandparents. She just looked so sad, and I wanted to make her happy, so of course, I would go to make her happy and then subject myself with a beating in the front seat of the car behind the Bowlerama. She did not want to wait until we arrived home. Why? Because I embarrassed her by first not wanting to go with her. I did not know I was embarrassing her. A mother's love is to be valued. It is something that you must work on continually, or so I thought. Now I realize not all mothers know how to be a mother. A mother's love sets the tone for all relationships. It has been a long road and the non-relationship I had with my mother affected how I raised my son and cared for all the women around me. I am indeed protective because I know how it feels to be unprotected by the one who is supposed to protect you. I know how it feels to be unloved and unwanted and I will never let anyone around me I care about feel those two things.

This is a story about unconditional love. I wish I could have a relationship with my mother. I know I may never, and, in that case, I must acknowledge that she will be fine, and I will be better.

MY FIRST BROKEN HEART DID
NOT COME FROM A LOVE
INTEREST.

21

JUST BEING

Today is the day I start just being. Today is the day that I finally came to grips with the understanding that the battle I have been fighting has already been fought and won and I need to just be. I will stop being anxious and I will stand firm in what I say. With that, I have the understanding that my mind can change in what I stood firm in a day ago because growth can happen. I give myself permission to just be myself in a world where everyone is trying to be someone else. I give myself permission to forgive all the hurt that I have done to myself. I permit myself to be free of all these societal guidelines and just BE. Just being is a lifestyle that others will hate you for. My life of just being has been questioned constantly. When my lifestyle used to come into question, I would transform into what society says I am, leaving me mad at myself for giving in. I am what I am, meaning you may not get what you see. Because what you see is your perception of me. You will get my perception of me, my love of me, the grace I have for me.

If I do not understand who I am, I will never have the capacity to understand who I can be.

If I do not respect my past, I will continue to struggle in my future.

I used to fear love. I used to fear real love. I ran away from love. I dreamed of love without dysfunction. When I received it, I did not think I was worth it. I doubted my ability to love. Love was a light shining through the blinds that I would never open. I feared the light. Although it warmed me, it gave me comfort, it allowed me to just be. I gave myself permission to just be. Just be in love with me.

FYI: the day this journal entry was written I was fired from my job. I guess for just being me.

I GIVE MYSELF PERMISSION TO LIVE MY LIFE OUT LOUD.

22

A BEAUTIFUL BOLD MESS

Once upon a time I would brag about being a beautiful bold mess, glorifying the fact that I was just a mess to hide the struggle I had going on in my spirit. My mind was all over the place not thinking straight, doing five tasks at once, completing them all telling people "I been so busy." At that time, all was not well with my spirit. I was struggling with a chaotic spirit which took time to uproot. Then I came to know peace within myself and understanding the importance of a healthy balance and that is when the transformation began.

Healing is transformational. That neurotic and dysfunctional part of myself will always be there. It is for me not to give life to it. It is how I remain safe from suffering and advance the love I have within me. Still beautiful and bold, just without the mess.

I RELEASE THE NEGATIVE
ENERGY THAT HAS BEEN
WEIGHING ME DOWN.

I AM REFRESHED AND
RENEWED.

23

LIFE IS TOO SHORT PERIOD.

Life is too short to constantly wonder "why?"

Life is too short to keep saying "what if."

Life is too short for me to keep agreeing for the sake of an argument.

Life is too short to keep accepting sorry every time I put up with some nonsense because of an explanation of "you know how I am."

Life is too short for me to brag about how someone deals or puts up with my chaotic behavior.

Life is too short to be complacent with the MESS, period. Mine or anyone else's.

The present is an instance between the past and the future, and I must live life in the present at this very moment.

Life is too short to wait for the past to catch up to my present.

Life is too short to keep holding on to something that let go of me.

I had to let go and open my hands so I could catch my blessings.

I had to move on so I could break free.

LIVE.

24

APPLYING ME COST ME

When I started to live in my truth, my vision became clear, and obstacles were cleared from my path. By applying the truth, I unlocked my freedom from within. I knew the joy of my freedom would cost me some people in my life and I did not care.

Well, it did cost me people. It taught people how to respect me. People know that I go from zero to one hundred quick. For years people would say things just so they could see that. One day I found out that I was a running joke for decades and even the babies were in on it. So, as I talk about living in my truth and vision being clear, just know that also brings discernment.

So, back to me being the running joke. It was this one day when every sentence said to me was said to provoke me, and with every sentence thrown at me I had an extremely sweet rebuttal. It was not hard as my granny said, "Kill them with kindness" because at this point in my life I was shifting for the better and it felt good. Finally, after they saw that I was not giving in to the slick remarks, they told me that I was a running joke. I politely ended the conversation. Yes, I was upset, and I thought about how these people could say they love me and want the best for me yet encouraging an ongoing joke about me. Making me livid so they could laugh and talk about me. I was mad as hell because a lot of people disliked me because of the anger I expressed toward these very people. I would be enraged to the point where there would sometimes be tears of hostility streaming down my face. That is how hard they would push my buttons, and it was all a joke. I was the joke.

* * *

That thing called grace. I remembered it. I was no longer that hurt person that let people push my buttons until I exploded. I was no longer that person who would just go along with the jokes that were harmful and disrespectful to me. I was now mentally stable and living in my resilient zone in peace.

EVERYWHERE I GO, I ARRIVE
UNAPOLOGETICALLY AS MY TRUE
SELF.

25

SMILING THROUGH MY "WHAT IF'S"

I once had the audacity to misplace myself in a world whose passage from one place to another was driven by a puffed-up sense of self-importance. Not only that, but I also had to meet benchmarks that were set by some unknown individuals to be judged by the world. This left me with a lack of conviction and uncertainty within myself. I was told I was already limited in my growth because I started a family at a young age. So, going away to college to hang out with a certain crowd to find a man to marry by a certain age to have children with, was out the door. I had to take a step back and ask, "How did I get here?" By following standards, I knew I wanted to destroy since I was six.

I knew in dance class when they tried to make me wear a pink tutu with my pink leotards to look identical to everyone else. Whatever this was, I was not having it. I did not wear a pink tutu. I revolted then, so what was I doing now? I had to ask myself, "What do I want for myself?" I just want to be filled with joy, to love and be loved with no limits, to write, and to travel. The same thing I wanted growing up. The illusion that I created in my mind was set by the world's standards and my failures. I was left feeling incompetent, unworthy, and in competition with others. Living in a life of chaos and forcibly smiling through my "what if's." I was suffering from memories of events that never took place. I was remembering ghost events for a period that I could not and would not let go of. Because they said I could have had that life, but I cannot now. I lost myself listening to the people who told me who I could and would be. The illusion that I created in my mind that kept me smiling through my "what ifs" was set by the world's standards for me. These standards were set unconsciously, adapted from the environment, and indoctrinated into me by others. They said I am a failure and that everything I try I will fail because I made a mistake too early in life to rectify.

If I am expected to fail, I better fail to abide by their rules. I have now failed to remember the standards they set for me and have created my own. Breaking free of false identity and not only smiling but sticking my middle finger up to the what ifs.

FAILURE IS A TEST OF FAITH,
NOT A DESTINATION.

26

FOREVER CHANGING

I had to grow and get out of what I called a pit.

I knew that some people would feel betrayed that I felt a change was necessary. When I left behind a place for new beginnings some thought I was expressing that something is wrong with the place I was leaving and the people there. I just wanted to break tradition for me and pursue a level of wholeness. It was about my growth as a person. That concept is only meant for me to grasp.

I am the earth—forever changing and growing . . . we all are, it just looks different for everyone. Some can grow where they are planted and some must uproot, plant, and grow somewhere else. Growth is forever changing. Change for me means exploration of myself and rising above the limits I set for myself. I woke up one day longing for the gifts I was born with, the ones that made me different, the extraordinary ones that manifested in my spirit. The gifts that growing up I lost sight of. The ones that enabled me to change.

I started taking advantage of change. It was a struggle mentally and physically, but I embraced it, worked through it, cried through it, laughed through it, went through it. I have unlearned and learned through it. I am impressed with the strength born out of my weakness. I love the peace that dwells inside me. I adore the patience I sit with in the place of anxiety. Change must happen for true learning to occur. Change in my behavior gave me new freedoms and highlighted the gifts bestowed upon me.

I am always prepared now because change is inevitable. Life has been evidenced to take a right when we are going left or vice versa. My primary job is to be willing, ready, and able to change and move forward when that time arrives. Nothing lasts, so I will be ready when the time comes when I must change and adjust again. When change occurs, I do not get upset, I just keep moving forward and be on the lookout for new provisions.

I am welcoming more change. I am requiring more change. Being comfortable crippled me. Being uncomfortable enabled my change. Growth is a requirement of change.

We need not only answers, we need problems too. It is only through the process of accepting and working through the problems that my ability to think creatively is enhanced, my persistence is stretched, and my self-confidence is deepened. Just like my body will not grow strong without being challenged to the point of exertion, it is the same with mind and spirit.

I challenge myself to grow. That is the goal: to always work on my growth as I change for the betterment of me.

IT IS NEVER TOO LATE TO
CHANGE DIRECTION.

27

WALKING BY FAITH

I once purchased a journal called "Walking by Faith." I purchased it in hopes of walking in faith. At the time I purchased the book, I had recently started my walk with faith and that walk was feeling delightful. I had not been obedient to my faith as I was dangerously listening to a lot of outside noise. Noises that I knew I should shut out. If I shut the noise out, I would then be considered 'acting new'. So, I gave up on faith, not for too long though. A couple of days after that, on March 22, 2006, I woke up and wrote in my journal: I am still existing. If I am still existing, I have a life to live.

I was sad, incredibly sad, though to the world I appeared happy. The world was demanding and not good to me. Karma was running behind me, and life was routine. That day, I said I must start searching for peace in my existence. From that moment on I started talking with intention.

Talk with intention and people will call you crazy. It was cool though. I had a purpose and I just had to walk with faith again, follow through. I could do it. As I started my walk back with faith, I learned that forgiveness is an act of faith. Once I forgave, I stopped reliving the situation. As I forgave, I felt a sense of freedom and strength within me. In forgiving, I learned to be mindful of my time.

Just ask how much time you spend thinking about words you said or events that happened that you cannot take back or you wish did not happen. Too much time. Apologize intentionally and move on. It did not matter if the person did not accept my apology. The apology was for me. Taking responsibility for my thoughts and actions completely.

* * *

I started setting reminders along with my daily intentions every day so I could grow and evolve into who I am and am becoming.

REMINDERS:

I deserve happiness.

My happiness is not selfish.

Practice aggressively living my life in the present moment and make it a habit.

Condition my mind for success.

BE honest with myself and alignment will begin to take place in my mind, body, and heart.

At all times, think happy thoughts.

I am healthy.

I am happy.

I am the truth.

I am love.

I am success.

I am good.

I will not attack my *I AM* in hopes of making others feel good. I am responsible for myself and myself alone.

Shift my thinking.

Shift my emotions.

Shift my attitude.

Gradually shift to a new position.

Stop procrastinating and make room for the shift.

Living in my truth is a repellent to unwanted strife.

Give time and attention to a daily action that will keep me moving forward.

I will not create a small space for me out of the way of others. I will take up the whole space and commit to space so I will have more space when it is time to expand.

What if I share space with a friend, family member, or coworker and their space is filled with chaos, confusion, clutter, and disorder? I will discontinue that shared space, not try to make it better. I will move without explanation.

My wins come from direct thoughts.

My peace comes from direct thoughts.

I cherish my visions and ideas; I will not forget that sometimes my visions and ideas may change with my growth and that is okay.

I desire peace and more life.

Balance leads to wholeness and wholeness leads to peace.

I am content with what and who I am, knowing that I will receive more.

If you ever see me talking to myself don't worry, I am reminding myself who and what *I am* and that I deserve it all.

I WILL CONTINUE TO WALK IN
FAITH.

28

KARMA GIVES YOU BACK WHAT YOU PLACE OUT IN THE WORLD

They say Karma is a bitch. Well, I say Karma can be my best friend if I go through life with good intentions. Karma is just a direct reflection of what you place out there in the universe. "What comes around goes around," as the saying goes. When we hear the word *karma*, we automatically think of something damaging. That is not the case.

As I read through my journals, I relived heartache, financial loss, pain, and a lot of tears, with a couple of mentions of regret that I had for the decisions I made. I was proud of the decisions I made because they were selfless, and in each one I did not place myself first. If I made a bad decision, it was usually driven by a good intention and I took the responsibility for the decisions, good or bad, and continued to move through them. Every time I placed my life in the back seat of others by helping them, it placed me in the front seat getting prepared for another new beginning in life, to be on my way to my purpose, and then . . . uh-oh, here comes someone else, and again and again I would place myself in the back seat and into the trunk. Sometimes quietly helping someone as I placed myself in the trunk to be used by them, doing everything in my power for them that I could as I struggled to move from the back seat and maybe one day to the front seat again. The whole time Karma was saying, "I got this. . . . Be still," and again thrusting me to the front seat and bringing my purpose to the forefront.

Back then, I never thought I deserved the front seat in what life was giving me, so I happily took back seats and laid in the trunk sometimes because I thought I was not good enough. So, I would give everything I had to anyone to make them happy, whether it was mentally, physically, emotionally, or financially. Time and time again life would replace what I gave away or lost and I would somehow give those things away again. Why? Because I did not deserve to be happy. I was not supposed to be happy; it was not in the stars for me because I was a teenage parent. I deserved to struggle because I made a mistake, and that is what was supposed to happen. Ironically, when I was out of the climate of what I would call the "cave" I was filled with joy. At least three times a week I would write down my priorities, a financial plan, write my resume over, look back at what I secretly accomplished, planning for me and Timmy's future and that excitement led me to singing wildly loud at night and dancing to the beat of my drums, off beat. Being crazy, cursing, being one with my poppy until I would laugh so hard I would fall asleep. My future filled me with joy and promise and that alone was forbidden because again I did not deserve it. Being told that repeatedly psychologically impacted me. At a certain point I knew I deserved the life karma kept giving me, but I kept letting opportunities pass me by because, in my weak mind, I did not want to let the people down who set those low standards for me. They loved me when I was down, so I had to stay down so they would continue loving me. I was a part of them. If I had gone beyond the standards they set for me, I was lied about, talked about, made to feel less than, and their standards were reiterated. I was not good enough and never would be, so stop it. There were many concerted efforts to cripple me mentally so I could not prosper in any way and that contributed to my mentality for a long length of time. My heart never stopped yearning to help others because I believed everyone deserves a chance. Yet my problem was that I did not think I deserved a chance. So, I gave everyone second, third, one hundred chances.

One day, I finally welcomed karma, understanding I deserve everything karma has given me because what I placed out in the universe was most times from a place of love and was intended to help others so they would not feel as lost and alone as I did. Getting laid off, getting fired, getting thrown out of the house on multiple occasions, being locked up, and everything I thought was detrimental to the annihilation of my mind, body, and spirit elevated me beyond what I ever imagined or wrote in my journals. I finally welcomed what the universe was trying to give me.

OUR LIVES ARE LIKE A BOOMERANGS, WHAT WE PLACE OUT IN THE UNIVERSE COMES RIGHT BACK.

MIND YOUR THOUGHTS, MIND YOUR WORDS, AND MIND YOUR ACTIONS.

29

CHALLENGES, STRUGGLES, LIFE

Life for me has always been a struggle internally. My internal struggles were roadblocks until I found out they were like a hurdle, waiting there for me to jump them or turn around and not even try. I think they were tests to see if I would stay in the comfortability of this life or if I would jump and break through the struggle to get to the place to mentally grow. I decided to jump.

Metaphorically it was not until my intuition guided me. I jumped figuratively, deciding to grow into who I was destined to be. I chose not to be a victim of my circumstances—I did not want to settle and stop living. I wanted life. A fulfilling life. I chose to be master of my universe where I would create a lifetime of joyous moments living in the richness and beauty that the universe was offering me. I changed my perception, and that is when the internal struggle ended. I was no longer fighting me or questioning me. No more obstacles, just my willingness to yield to the universe. I feel I am unstoppable because I know my only limit is myself. When I thought there was too much to handle it was just me lacking stability because of my insecurities. I could not manage my time because I could not manage my mind. The doubts and fears managed the struggle for me.

Giving up the struggle made me softer, more balanced, able to be at ease and happy. I was stronger mentally, because I gave up the facade of being strong, making more space for gratitude and forgiveness to settle in.

I lived an arduous, complicated life.

I lived through it by overcoming life experiences and rising to multiple occasions. I rose because I kept telling myself "Nothing can get worse than this, it only gets better, and the only place I am destined to go is up."

That is where I went. I ascended, transforming the pain to promise to bring me to a place of peace, knowing I can take on anything that comes my way. And if I fall, I get up and rise again. I learned that how many times I fall does not matter if each time I get back up. Each time I got back up I became wiser, more alert, more strategic, more willing to take risks, more self-assured, more patient, more confident in my abilities, more optimistic, more empowered, and more mindful in my approach to everyday life.

When I was at war with my soul, I did things despite what I knew the outcome would be. I said things to hurt others and I deflected on others what I felt inside about myself. I smiled, I laughed, and all the while on the inside I was struggling, internally breaking.

Intuition told me to surrender, and I will have peace. When I surrendered and started to have patience with myself that is when I conquered, overcame, and took total control of my situation. I began to face the truth while taking control and fully understanding my emotions because now I knew they were a factor in building character. Emotions affect how we feel, how we think, what we say, and what we do.

I RISE OUT OF TURMOIL, TRANSFERRING MY PAIN TO MY GIFTS,ENGULFING MYSELF IN A WORLD OF BEAUTY FOCUSING ON MAKING EVERY DAY BETTER.

30

CHILD-LIKE FAITH

I believe that when we are children, we dream about what our life will look like when we come to age. As we grow and change, we sometimes lose focus of those dreams. We start adapting to our surroundings, we adopt our peers' values and welcome their opinions. We stop honoring our dreams and honor the dreams of others. We are swayed by what is played on the television and radios, we are crushed by the word *no*, our hearts are broken, and the hopes and dreams fade into what we settle for.

I had to grow up fast because I had a baby at an early age. I kept a childlike faith though. It willed me through some of the roughest times of my life. When I was young, if someone told me I was going to get hurt doing something, I would not care. I would do it anyway. I thought it was fun. Or if they said, "That is for boys," again I was going to do it anyway. If my mom said to me, "You just had jazz and classical dance back-to-back. You can't wrestle." I would give my dad a look, letting him know that it was time to rumble. I let that child-like faith slip once upon a time, giving into external forces and conditioning. In a quiet place I discovered it again and I then made a promise to myself: I will never let it go again.

There have been plenty of times when my confidence was shaking. When I wanted to quit.

I reminded myself that I am no quitter and that I have faith.

As a child, when I fell off a bike, I quickly picked the bike back up, jumped on it, and took off riding to my destination.

I could have just gripped the handlebars, and admired the color and paint while I walked the bike, yet avoiding the pain of falling or failure again?

I did not walk it. I got back on and rode.

If I did not get back on, I would have never experienced the feel of the wind in my face, the strength of my core creating balance, the calmness of my mind as the adrenaline flowed through my body as I released my hands off the handlebars and raised my arms as if I were flying. That is child-like faith.

A world of adventure begins with the courage to take one risky step of faith over that bicycle bar. To grip the handlebars, sit down, and lift our feet off the ground—determined to push the pedals forward once more.

NEVER LOSE THAT CHILD-LIKE
FAITH.

31

GRACE

I always pray for grace. With grace, letting go and forgiving came with ease. To have and to hold and to extend grace through life. I extend grace through trying my best to do everything in love. That is why everything I do is to the best of my ability. If you ask me a question, I will tell you all I know, and how I came to find out the answer. And if I am not happy with the answer, I will give you resources to find the answer. I support my friends in their endeavors and offer them advice and resources. My conversations are important because, when the conversation is over, I want that person to know that I am listening and that I am aware, and they have a safe place with me in love. I AM intentional and I have a lot of passion about everything I do, even the minor things because it is all done in grace with love.

I extend grace so that the next person may grow in grace. I am learning not to question a person's why's. I have learned that the extension of grace shows an understanding of love. Grace allows us to accept things as they are and to love without judgment. We all have faults. We all deserve forgiveness, and we all have the honor to extend grace if we choose to.

We are all human, we all have flaws, and knowing this we should always lead with grace.

HE forgives, and I also heard we all are justified freely by his grace through the act of redemption. Grace had been bestowed upon me, so I pay it forward by bestowing grace upon others.

LOVE AND GRACE CLEANSES THE INNER WOUNDS AND HEALS THE SOUL.

32

SHOTS OF INSPIRATION

I believe in me.
  I believe in my gifts.
  I believe in my abilities
  I believe they are worth the time to bring them to pass, to make them happen, to see them come true.

I WILL RISE TO GREATNESS, LETTING GO OF ALL THAT IS HOLDING ME BACK.

I WILL LET MY IMAGINATION RUN WILD AS I RUN AFTER MY DREAMS USING MY GIFTS AND ABILITIES.

33

YESTERDAY IS GONE

Yesterday is gone. I should have neither fear nor worry about yesterday because it has passed, left me forever with no way to return. Yesterday is now beyond my control. I cannot bring back yesterday, I cannot undo a single act I performed, and I cannot erase a single word I said. Yesterday is gone forever.

What I can do tonight is pray that tomorrow will be better than yesterday and speak productivity, love, and passion into existence for tomorrow. Shout that tomorrow will be great. Shout that I will live tomorrow to the fullest. I let the Gods know that tomorrow is the day that my dreams will come true, and I will win in life because I declared it.

I AM NOT CONCERNED ABOUT RECTIFYING THE PAST. MY CONCERN IS NOT LIVING IN IT ANYMORE.

34

OCCUPY MY MIND
WITH SUCCESS

Doubt was another one of my dream killers, so think positive. My thoughts are what motivates me to succeed or not to succeed. My success is supported by my thoughts, so I do not let doubt creep into my mind and take over my thoughts anymore. Leave no room for doubt. I occupy my mind with all the wonderful and fabulous experiences that are happening in my life along with the enthusiasm of the process of completing my goals. I know that I am strong enough to succeed and I remember: failure leads to success, but it is doubt that kills it. You can fail twenty times, but those twenty failures will come together and make one big success. Never leave room for doubt, even if you fail.

ONCE I SURRENDERED TO THE SPIRIT OF TRUTH THERE WAS NO LONGER ROOM FOR DOUBT IN MY HEART.

35

THE BEST IS YET TO COME

I cannot always control the story of my life. Sometimes things happen that are beyond my control. We all have other characters that play a part in our lives, and we do not control them or nature. So, whatever happens, I face it head on and always remember there is a reason for everything. What I must do is make the best out of every situation. That is the battle I fight. I used to look for the worst in life so I could be prepared for whatever may happen, and if it happens to be good it just happens. I changed my thinking and no longer prepare for the worst.

If you think about it and let it manifest in your mind, it will happen. Think about greatness, think about a fun-filled and joyful life. Do not prepare for the worst, look forward to the best. Prepare for the best and you will have the best. You can redesign your life by transforming your mind.

MY LIFE ONLY GETS BETTER.

36

DECISIONS

I am what I am today because of the decisions I made every day leading up to today.

I started beginning each day with a blueprint of my values firmly planted in my mind. So, when those hard challenges and situations came, I could make the right decisions based on those values instead of the emotion in the moment.

Keep a cool head, and if I happen to make the wrong decision in life it is okay. I will use it as a teaching moment to keep building my foundation. It is those teachable moments that I take responsibility for because of my values, which enables me to grow and mature to become a better decision maker.

When I take responsibility for my failures as well as my successes, I have—right there in those moments—decided to stand bold in my decisions. I have no regrets and I keep moving forward. Taking responsibility for my decisions helps me build my character.

The power of change is in the decisions I make and the words that I speak. That awareness is what leads me to change. To get to the person I am today, I have struggled with life and societal norms that have affected me in some way or another. I have surpassed that and am moving forward, using my creative abilities to nurture and grow my skills

with who I am. The confidence I now have in myself expresses itself
through the decisions I make and how I navigate through life.

I AM CONFIDENT, PASSIONATE, AND INTENTIONAL ABOUT THE DECISIONS I MAKE.

37

I DO NOT EXIST JUST TO SURVIVE

I am not just existing. I am living and not just to survive. No day is just another day. It is a brand-new day, a chance for us to shine, and shine bright. We have the sun that rises every morning to remind us of that. Every day, every hour, every minute, every second I have the power to continuously change—I have the earth to remind me of that. I am constantly changing. I choose to continuously move forward because that backward direction had me trippin'. Even on my dark days when I am going through different emotions, no need to go backward, light will always shine even in the darkest of times. I have the moon to remind me of that. This is my life to decree and declare that I am worthy of whatever I want. I have the right to let go and move on. I do not need permission from anyone. I have passion, purpose, and gifts. My contribution to life is valuable and I choose to live inside my purpose. I choose to share my gifts because I am becoming aware of me. I am tapping into my power. All because I chose me, regardless of how much I tripped. I kept walking in my purpose until those baby steps of small intensity quietly transcended into a power walk.

That is all it took. I just kept moving forward, not even in a loud, boastful way . . . just quietly, in slow motion, savoring each moment of my journey.

I NEVER HAVE TO CATCH UP
BECAUSE I AM NOT JUST
EXISTING, I AM LIVING EVERY
DAY TO THE FULLEST AS I
CHANGE, MATURE, AND GROW
CREATING A BETTER ME.

38

LOVE IS IN THE DETAILS

Love is jumping in the bed between my granny and poppy, turning my head to the right side to give my poppy a goodnight kiss then turning to the left side and giving my granny a goodnight kiss, saying our prayers together and then they both doze off to sleep while I am talking.

Love is lathering up a washcloth and gently, in circular motions, washing your granny's back as she speaks quietly to you about the luxury of taking time out to care for yourself and rest, and about how the absence of sound, at times, can be beneficial.

Love is sitting at the legs of your poppy's chair as he reads the newspaper and then passes it to you to read the same words to him that he just read to himself. He would always remind me how important it is to read every day.

Love is sitting in between your aunt or cousin's legs as they part your hair with a comb as they gently grease your scalp, then take your hair in between their fingers to braid.

Love is riding down I-95 to Baltimore, sitting in the front seat between your mom and your dad, singing to the top of your lungs "Let's Hear It for the Boys."

Love is standing next to your mom's white vanity table and chair as she gives herself three squirts of a pleasantly smelling perfume, then squirts you. She then puts her lipstick on then puts the same lipstick on me and says, "Pucker your lips."

Love is getting picked up by your dad every weekend and driving around Delaware and to Pennsylvania to play numbers, get the latest Nikes and fried chicken.

Love is wildly dancing in your uncle's room to Earth Wind & Fire and him patiently (but his friends impatiently) waiting for the entire record to go off so he can go outside.

Love is sharing with my son the same prayer I used to say with my poppy and granny every night before bedtime. It is what will keep us close and grounded. Love is changing the lyrics to "Kissing You" by Total to "Missing you" and singing them to my son before sending him off to school . . . "You're my pride and joy, you're my baby boy. People ask me how I feel 'bout you. They ask me if I miss you. Missin' you is all that I have been thinking of. Missin' you."

LOVE EXPRESSES ITSELF IN
MANY FORMS. TO FIND IT
SOMETIMES YOU MUST PAY CLOSE
ATTENTION TO THE DETAILS.

39

JUST HEALING AS I AM WRITING.

To heal, I had to understand that living in my truth was vital to thrive in life. I had to understand not to be ashamed of my truth because that truth is what made me. To heal, I had to realize that my foundation was cracked in some areas. That is okay. The foundation that was not cracked guaranteed me the stability to rise and be able to love, understand, and forgive.

I had to let go of the past, knowing I was moving at a pace of now and that, whatever is happening now, is where my focus should lie. In allowing myself to practice presence, I have more love and compassion for myself, enabling me to open that space up for others. I leave one minute to live in this minute, not thinking about—although unconsciously setting me up—for the next minute. Enjoying now by experiencing now with all my senses honoring me in the present state. Whatever emotions come I sit with them, allowing myself to understand them, and move through them. My *I am love* thoughts may falter here and there. Then I remember I cannot waste my now and, at this moment, I know that I am good enough for me. Usually, my faltering comes from living in the past and being told I am not good enough. I am good enough. I cannot worry about others or why they think the way they do. I just have to have compassion for them with the understanding that I know we are all worthy of love. I must remind myself of that sometimes.

These writings are for inspiration and motivation, not instruction. I write because I am determined to be a better person. I am not here to constantly reread what I did wrong so I could feel bad about myself. I am here to reread what I have done so I can do better. These writings are to light the way to change, to monitor how far I have come. They are reminders telling me to let go and move on.

I do not make my words pretty. I just tell the truth about me. The truth is beautiful and enlightening and damaging and heartless and undeniable and heart-wrenching. It is also healing, and for me, truly represents the love I have for myself and it cannot be changed. Truth is, I still have a lot of stuff to work through and I am continuously trying to figure me out. Through those continuous emotional tears of joy, not sadness at all, just tears of joy that invades my face when I am enlightened . . . for that, I will continue living my best life.

I am the words I speak.

I am forgiving.

I am forgiven.

I am enough.

I am joy.

I am love.

I am healing.

I am Kishna Marie.

I own it.

I personalize it.

I embody it.

CPSIA information can be obtained
at www.ICGtesting.com
Printed in the USA
LVHW022231041021
699496LV00016B/638